The Calligrapher's Handbook

NEW
BURLINGTON
BOOKS

Monday's child is fair of face,
Tuesday's child is full of grace,
Wednesday's child is full of woe,
Thursday's child has far to go,
to attend

calligraphy class

Friday's child is loving and giving,
Saturday's child works hard for its living,
But the child that is born on the
Sabbath day, Is bonny, and blithe,
and good, and gay.

CONTENTS

First published in 1987 by
New Burlington Books
6 Blundell Street, London N7 9BH

Copyright © 1987 Quintet Publishing Limited

ISBN: 1 85348 116 5

Reprinted 1989

Printed and bound in Hong Kong

WHAT IS CALLIGRAPHY?

In order to understand and participate in the subject, the word calligraphy must be defined. The dictionary states 'handwriting or penmanship', or simply 'beautiful handwriting'. My own definition is much tighter and reads 'letters produced by the means of a square-ended implement'. This includes quill pens, reed pens, metal pens, brushes, felt- or fibre-tip pens and even a piece of card or wood – in fact, anything with a square end capable of producing an image on a variety of surfaces by leaving an ink or medium deposit.

The earliest evidence of a written hand is a limestone tablet of around 3500 BC, which is made up from pictograms. These developed into ideograms – pictures to represent ideas or less definite objects. Finally phonograms were used – these were symbols representing sounds.

However, the roots of our present-day letters are to be found in the Roman alphabet of the first century AD. These majuscule, or capital, letters were mainly for incising into stone with a chisel and I believe that they owe their shape to this fact. The best-known surviving example of Quadrata, or Square Capital, lettering is an inscription to be found at the foot of Emperor Trajan's Column in Rome, AD 114. This fine, chiselled lettering is held to be a model for all artists to follow. It has certainly stood the test of time, although there is some conjecture as to the production of this work. It has been suggested that the letters were formed initially by a lettering artist with a brush and then cut by a stone craftsman. The style of the lettering, however, reflects more the action of the chisel than that of the brush, especially when considering the fine serifs, which form the ends of the main strokes of the letters. In order to cut lettering into stone, the V-groove chisel starts at the surface and cuts into the material to form the deeper channel of the main stroke. It would almost appear that the serifs (letter beginnings and endings) became an essential part of the process, later being squared off to form a cap and foot to the letter.

The Romans used a second main style called Rustica. This was a less formal, more fluid, letterform than Quadrata and was principally produced with a pen or a brush. It is more elongated than Quadrata, and this, coupled with its flowing form, made it an economical style to use in books as more writing could be contained within a page. There were other decorative Roman styles but they have little relevance in this book.

Calligraphers and letter designers are still emulating the incised square capital. Much of this can be ascribed to the evolution from one style to another and much to tradition. However, the very shape of a square-ended implement utilized in producing letterforms naturally dictates its own starting and ending points, thus negating the need for an additional serif, which must be regarded as adornment only. Many styles said to have evolved through a desire for speed are unbelievably elaborate for their intended purpose. If speed were of the essence, surely the fewer the strokes, the more efficient the style. It must therefore be accepted that calligraphic forms are rarely written for ease and with communication as the prime factor: more often than not, artistic appearance is given priority over legibility.

This book reflects both traditional and modern styles, but with the emphasis on legibility and practical usage when compiling alphabet samples.

An example of the informal style, 'Rustica.'

Modern incised lettering.

4

NOMENCLATURE

In order to discuss the subject of letters, calligraphers, letter designers and students require terminology to describe the constituent parts of letterforms. When analyzing a particular style, this nomenclature is used to define the various elements in a concise manner. There is no standard nomenclature to define constituent parts of letters but many of the terms are self-explanatory. The terminology used here is based on that employed by letter designers and therefore may differ from that found in calligraphic references. Many descriptions are repeated from letter to letter as these terms are used generally throughout the alphabet and are not necessarily confined to a specific letter. The parts and names illustrated refer to the Quadrata capitals (majuscule) and a complementary lower-case (minuscule) alphabet although most of the terms can be employed to define other forms.

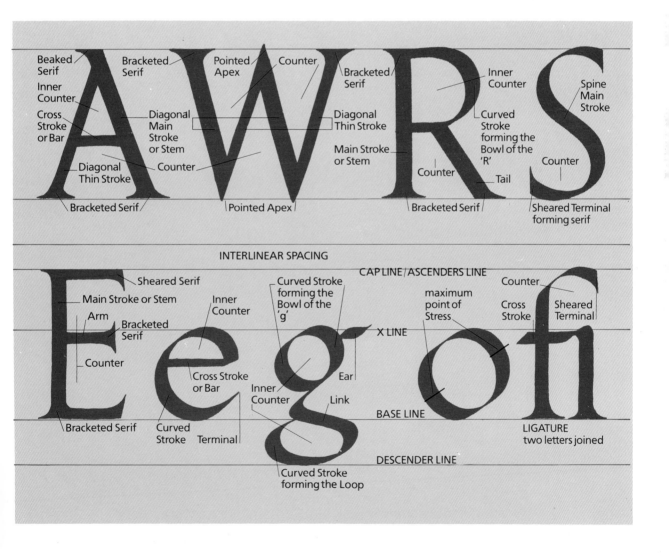

5

MATERIALS AND TOOLS

The craft of calligraphy does not require a large outlay: the main requirements are pen, ink and paper, and the main ingredient is a willingness to learn. Don't rush out and buy any old pen. Read these pages carefully and then decide upon your own requirements.

There is a tremendous range of materials and implements available to the calligrapher. The craft is currently experiencing a revival and many companies are entering this market for the first time, especially in the production of writing implements. As this book is aimed at the newcomer, I have deliberately limited the material content to that which will be required in producing the samples in this book.

WRITING TOOLS

There are two main types of steel-nibbed pens: the pen nib with reservoir and pen holder, which requires constant filling, and the fountain-type pen, which has a built-in reservoir. The latter is, I feel, a better choice for the beginner. It relieves the student of the tedious task of constantly refilling the reservoir, using a paint brush or pipette which then requires washing out, before continuing to letter; full concentration is needed and so any distraction or encumbrance should be avoided.

Whichever type of pen is chosen always inform the supplier whether it is for a right- or left-handed person. There are special nibs for left-handed users where the end of the nib slopes top right to bottom left when viewed from the top. Whichever pen collection is chosen, there will be a variety of nib sizes available, although the size of, say, an italic fine nib may vary between different manufacturers, whether it is for a fountain pen or nib holder.

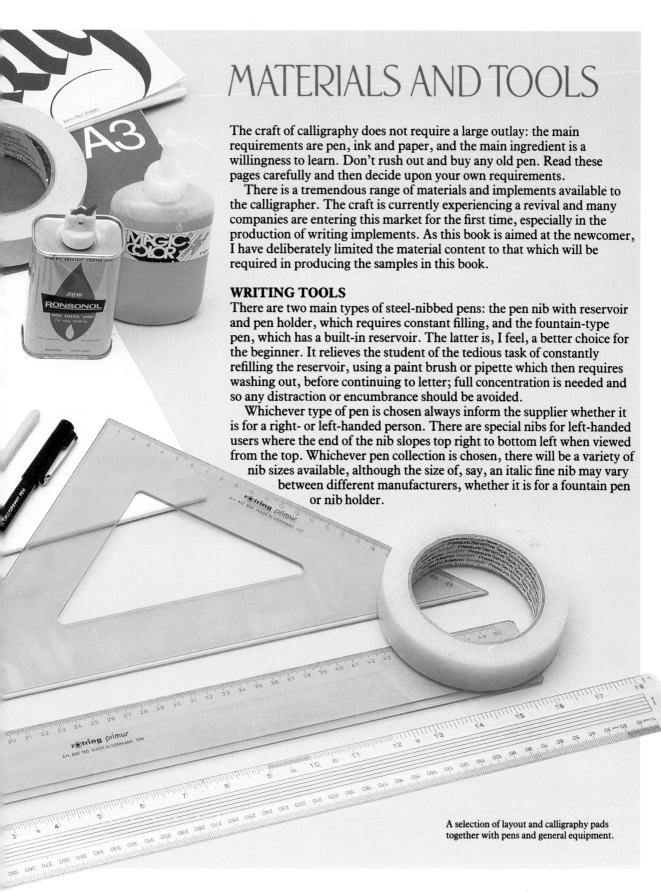

A selection of layout and calligraphy pads together with pens and general equipment.

Left and right hand nib units.

Fountain-type pens

There are various calligraphic pens on the market. Some are purchased as an integral unit (that is, a complete pen); others are bought as a set and include a barrel, reservoir and a set of interchangeable nib units.

Don't be afraid to ask the local art shop or stationers to show their entire range. The larger suppliers often have demonstration pens that can be tested before finally making a decision to purchase.

The choice of pens available is ever-increasing and I have used many different makes of pen. The one on which I have become reliant and have used since my college days is an Osmiroid. It suits my style and I feel comfortable using it. However, the choice is yours.

The ink holders, or reservoirs, are of either the squeeze or piston type and all three pens have an optional cartridge ink supply..

Pen holders and inks

Once the student has gained confidence and experience with a pen, a pen holder and range of nibs is the next addition to any calligrapher's equipment. The range available is vast, including round-hand, script, poster, scroll and special-effect nibs. These items are sold separately or can often be bought on a display card which contains pen holder, reservoir and set of nibs. If a student does decide to purchase this type of pen he will need to remove the film of lacquer with which the nibs are coated to avoid deterioration. This can be done either by passing the nib through a flame briefly or by gently scraping the surface.

A selection of nibs and holders.

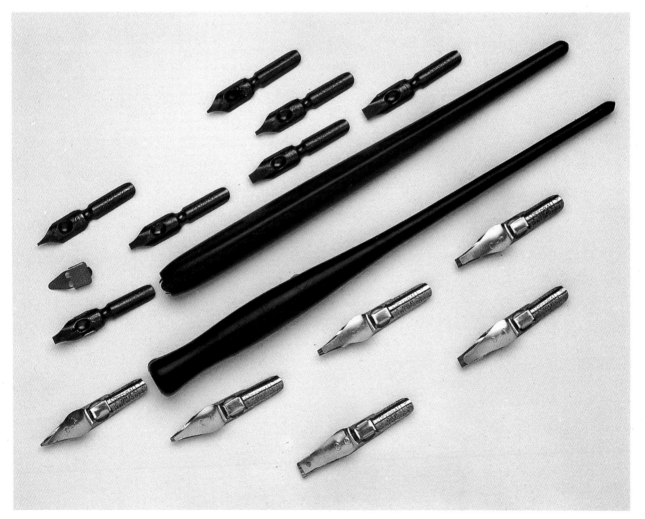

INKS

There are many inks available to the student, and choice is made difficult by this fact. The main property an ink should have is that it should flow easily and not clog the pen. Non-waterproof ink flows marginally better than waterproof inks and watercolours. The medium should not spread on the writing surface. Unwanted feathering can be attributed either to the paper or to the ink, and the student should experiment with both to confirm compatibility.

Density of colour is important in finished work, and there are inks available which are specifically stated as being calligraphic inks. These are suitable for use in fountain-type pens. There are also inks that are referred to as 'artist colour', some of which are waterproof; many need a cleaning fluid to clean or flush the pen through after use. (Check with the stockist that such a cleaning agent will have no harmful effects.) The range of colours is wide, and most of these types of ink are miscible, giving an even wider range.

Calligraphers often use watercolour paint for embellishment. This is satisfactory for a pen and holder but not for a fountain pen. Instead of watercolour, pens can be filled with artists' retouching dye, which is translucent and the colour is very pure and water soluble. Ink and watercolours vary in light fastness; so check the label for the product's degree of permanence.

Some bottles have a pipette incorporated in the cap. This is useful for charging the reservoirs in pen holders and saves loading with a brush.

PAPER

For the beginner, a draughtsman's or designer's layout pad is ideal for roughing out ideas and preliminary penwork. Pads come in various sizes, finishes and weights. Initially, choose a paper that is not too opaque and make sure, when the paper is placed over the sample alphabets in this book, that you can still see the letterforms through it.

There are typo pads specifically made for designers' layouts. This type of pad is ideal, because it is used for tracing letters in studios when laying out work. It has a slightly milky appearance and is not as transparent as tracing paper.

For finished work a good quality cartridge paper is ideal. Writing papers are produced in many shades and finishes, although they can be a little restrictive due to the sizes available. There are also many drawing papers which can be put to good use. It is as well to experiment with different types of paper, avoiding those with a heavy coating, as they will obstruct the passage of the nib and the flow of the ink. For outdoor work such as posters, special papers that weather well can be used, but do not forget to use a waterproof ink.

Ingres paper for finished work, available in pads
or single sheets.

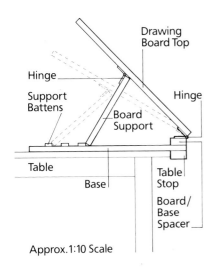

Drawing Board Top

Hinge

Support Battens

Hinge

Board Support

Table

Base

Table Stop

Board/ Base Spacer

Approx. 1:10 Scale

A home-made drawing board with three adjustable angles.

A Trueline drawing board with parallel motion.

DRAWING BOARD

A drawing board on which to work will of course be required. This need not be an expensive purchase. In calligraphy, work is carried out with the drawing board at an angle. The student should be positioned in front of the work so that he can see it clearly without stretching. The angle of the board should ideally be about 45°. However, providing the calligrapher is in a good viewing position, it may be as low as 30° – whatever suits the individual. Never work on a flat surface as this necessitates bending over the board and using the pen in an upright position, whereas on a sloping board the pen is at a shallower angle, helping to regulate the ink flow.

A drawing board can be purchased, with or without adjustable angles, from most art shops. Alternatively, laminate shelving board is available at most timber merchants and is quite adequate. A suitable board size is 18 × 24 in (450 × 600 mm). Apply iron-on laminate edges to give a clean finish. The board can be supported on one's lap and leant against a table or desk, making an angle of about 45° with the desk top. A professional-looking board that adjusts to three angles can be made quite readily. The board illustrated is approximately one-tenth scale and therefore all measurements will require multiplying by ten.

Cut two laminate boards to the dimensions above, one for the base and the other for the top. In the same material cut a further piece for the board support and some softwood for support battens, table stop and board-base spacer. All these items measure the same width as the drawing board. In addition six butt hinges and some chipboard screws will be required.

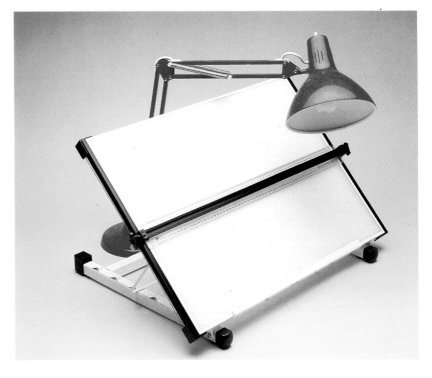

Screw a board spacer to one edge of the base together with a table stop on the opposite side to prevent the board from sliding when in use. Screw the support battens to the base in the positions shown to give three angles from 30° to 45° approximately.

Attach the board support to the drawing board top with three of the hinges, one in the centre and one a little distance in from each end. It is essential that the support is positioned correctly to achieve the desired angles. Fix the remaining three hinges to the drawing board, underside at the base, with the other side to the board-base spacer. Give all edges a clean finish with iron-on laminate.

RULER

Choose an 18 in (450 mm) ruler, preferably with both metric and imperial calibrations. Transparent rulers with grid lines running parallel to their edges can be useful for horizontal alignment in rough layouts, where multiple lines need ruling.

A ruler with a good bevelled edge is more accurate in transferring measurements and is useful when reversed for ruling ink lines as the bevelled edge prevents ink seeping under the ruler.

SET SQUARE

A 45° set square will be required. Some have millimetre calibrations on the right-angled edges, and these are useful when laying out rectangular shapes. The square should be at least 10 in (250 mm) on the two shorter edges. A smiliar 30°/60° set square will also be needed.

PENCILS

An H or 2H pencil is needed for preliminary guidelines, which need to be fine. The leads are not too soft; so the student won't be spending all his time keeping a keen point on the pencil.

An HB will be required for rough layout work as it is sufficiently soft to give a good image without unnecessary pressure. A soft carpenter's pencil is ideal for initial test layouts and can be sharpened to a chisel edge to emulate the size of calligraphic nib to be used.

Propelling, or clutch, pencils have become very popular in recent years, and HB, H and 2H leads are available. A ⅟₅₀ in (0.5mm) lead size is preferable, as the smaller leads tend to snap easily.

ERASER

There are many erasers on the market. Choose a plastic one for paper and film.

ROMAN SERIFED
ALPHABET

"I WILL GIVE YOU SEVEN YEARS OF FREEDOM," SAID THE DRAGON

"At the end of that time I will ask you a riddle. If you guess it the bargain is ended. But if you cannot guess it you must be my servants through all eternity"

This style is based on Edward Johnston's Foundational Hand, which was modified from a 10th-century manuscript. In construction it is similar to Roman Sans Serif, but with the addition of serifs to give the style its character. These serifs are formed either by a change of direction, as in the serif at the foot of the thin diagonal stroke of the 'A', or by a second curved stroke into the main stem, such as that at the cap line of the 'B'. There are also tapered terminals, which are formed by a curving of the stroke ending at the pen angle, giving a point. This can be seen in the main stem of the 'A'.

The alphabet is lettered at an angle of 30° throughout with the exception of the capitals 'N', 'X' and 'Z'. The angle for both vertical strokes of the 'N' has been changed to 45° to give a slightly thinner stroke. The thin diagonal stroke of the 'X' has been lettered at 15° from the horizontal in order to give the stroke some body and keep it more in line with the thin diagonal strokes of the 'V' and 'W'. The 'Z' is the only letter that, when lettered with a 30° angle, has a main diagonal stem which is less in weight than the horizontal strokes. I feel that this anomaly should be overcome and have therefore adjusted the angle to 15° from the horizontal to give the stroke some stature. The lower case 'z' also requires this change.

As a guide, if the main strokes of any letter are regarded as being the trunk of a tree, then all other strokes emanating from the stem should be of a weight that the main stem can support. This, I hope, explains my concern with the letter 'Z'. All these above adjustments have been made to give the letters concerned a better relationship with other characters – to achieve harmony and continuity.

However carefully the letterforms are drawn, there will undoubtedly be a slight deviation from the 30° angle. Provided that it is only minor, it will not measurably affect the end result.

The guidelines should be drawn as indicated at the top of the first page of the alphabet. The numerals fall within the x height area but the student can, if he wishes, increase the size to that of the capitals. However, I prefer them slightly smaller. Most of the characters are lettered with finger movement only, although the longer strokes may need some arm movement coming from the shoulder.

Once the alphabet in its present form has been mastered, the student may wish to letter the style in the following proportions.

	ascenders	x height	descenders
nib widths	2	4¼	2
nib widths	2½	5	2½

This exercise is well worth the effort as it will show how a letterform changes in character when minor proportional adjustments are made. The alphabet style should, nevertheless, retain its general appearance and flavour once the nib values are changed. The overall effect of the proportional changes would be to make a page of text appear lighter.

Capital height: 6 nib widths
This alphabet is lettered with a B4,
the metric equivalent being a 2·3mm.

Nib Angle approximately 30°

Arrows denote direction of stroke.
Numerals indicate order of character
construction.

Nib Angle changed to 45° for the
vertical strokes of the N.

Nib Angle changed to 15° for the diagonal stroke of the Z.

Nib Angle changed to 15° for the thin diagonal stroke of the X.

Ascenders: 2 nib widths

'x' height: 4 nib widths

Descenders: 2 nib widths

a a b b c c

c d e e f f

g g h h i i

j j k k l l

m m n n o o

p p q q r r

s s t t u u

v v w w

x x y y z z

30°

15°

GETTING STARTED

The student should now have a basic understanding of letter construction and the necessary tools and materials to commence calligraphic lettering. The styles compiled in the following sections are basic calligraphic forms, but this certainly does not mean that they are easy. The student will require determination, patience and, in order to maintain concentration, peace and quiet.

I intend to make the learning of the subject as simple as possible. I have, in my lessons at calligraphic class, cut the learning time down by employing methods that are not altogether accepted in some teaching circles. Nevertheless, the students I have worked with have achieved an awareness of letterforms and have made rapid progress, becoming proficient with a pen very quickly; I therefore hope that the learning principles laid down in this book are adhered to. If I ask for a certain standard to be maintained — for example, accurate laying out of guidelines for lettering — the instructions should be followed carefully: the use of blunt pencils to mark these out would be unacceptable because it would produce inaccuracies.

I am, therefore, asking for the student to 'go by the book'. Wherever possible, time-saving devices have been incorporated to assist progress. So do not try to take short cuts. This invariably ends up with the student having to back-track. I have tried to indicate where the student could go wrong, in order to avoid unexpected disappointment and encourage perseverance. Students experiencing problems should check that they

A card support with book in position for right-handed students.

A card support for left-handed students.

have followed the instructions correctly. I am convinced that most people can letter well, when properly guided.

SETTING UP THE DRAWING BOARD TO TRACE

The drawing board now has to be set up so that the book can be used as a tracing reference. Right-handed students should take a strip of heavy mounting card and position it with tape on to the writing surface. This is to rest this book on when the letterforms in the first sample are traced.

For left-handed students the card is positioned differently, because it is difficult for left-handed calligraphers to letter horizontally. The writing hand obscures the lettering produced and, even with a left-handed nib, to achieve the correct angle of writing can involve an uncomfortable pen hold. By tilting the paper the problem is lessened.

Therefore, left-handed students could try positioning the work with its right-hand side dropped down 15° from the horizontal, with the extra piece at right angles to prevent the book from sliding to the right. The student can then try lettering a few characters. If the position is uncomfortable the angle may need to be adjusted several times.

Once lettering exercise 1 has been tried, the student might find that by merely turning the paper through various degrees, he is still unable to achieve the desired angle of lettering. He should then resort to grinding down the nib to form an even steeper angle. This can be done on a fine-grade India stone or fine-grade production paper (the type used by car sprayers in the preparation of paintwork).

To save undue expense, experiment first with a nib used with a pen holder before attempting to convert a fountain-pen nib. This way, at least, if the result is not satisfactory, a relatively costly nib will not have been ruined. Make sure that when grinding down the edge, a burr is not left on one side, nor the edge left so sharp as to cut into the surface of the paper to be lettered. Finally, ensure that the edge of the nib is square, not rounded.

Applying padding to drawing board.

SETTING UP THE DRAWING BOARD FOR GENERAL WORK

Remove the pieces of card used to retain the book. Take two sheets of cartridge paper and cut them to a size which is 3 in (75 mm) less than the height and width of the surface area of the drawing board. If the board has been constructed from the illustration in this book, $15^3/_{16} \times 21$ in (385 × 535 mm) will be required. Place these sheets on the board surface with an equal border all around of about $1^1/_2$ in (40 mm). Using masking tape, stick both sheets together to the board. It will be easier if this is done with the board flat. Attach one of the long edges of the sheets first, then pull the sheets taut and stick down the opposite side. Then tape the two exposed ends.

For the pad cut a further, slightly larger, sheet of cartridge which will give a border of 1 in (25 mm) on the drawing board and stick this with tape on all four edges so that no edge is left exposed and the sheet is taut.

This will now provide an ideal writing surface. The pen does not perform well against a hard, solid surface and the backing sheets give a little spring, which is suited to the action of the nib. Once the students' first alphabet has been lettered, the student should have a good idea of the point on the board when he feels most comfortable when lettering. This position will differ with the individual and is known as the writing level.

To prevent grease from the hand being deposited on the writing sheet, make a guard sheet from a sheet of cartridge paper. It must be positioned with tape on to the pad at a level that allows the student to work on his writing line.

To retain the writing sheet as it is moved towards the top of the board at the end of each line of lettering, a strip of fabric tape or card may be used at the top of the board. This is an optional extra; I prefer the sheet to be mobile, but I do recognize the strip's value when writing on material that has a tendency to curl.

Always put aside a spare piece of the writing material being used to start the pen off and to practice strokes.

Applying cover to drawing board.

LIGHTING

Correct lighting is as important for the eyes as posture is for the limbs. Tired eyes and limbs are not conducive to clean, crisp calligraphy. Ideally the student should work in daylight. If he is right-handed, the light source should be from the left, and if left-handed, from the right. Light, correctly directed, should ensure that the calligrapher is not working in his own shadow cast by the writing hand. Lighting therefore plays a key role in the laying out of the working area. Strong direct light, such as sunlight, should be avoided, as excessive glare from the usual white surface being worked will make lettering difficult.

The student will also need artificial light from an anglepoise lamp or similar unit, either wall-mounted or standing. The direction of the source is the same as for daylight. The advantage of an anglepoise lamp is that of ease of direction or position; for intricate work, light can be directed to the point required by simple adjustment.

THE POSITION TO ADOPT WHEN LETTERING

It is important to be comfortable when seated, with the feet flat on the floor, the back straight and the drawing board positioned so that the arms can move freely.

The height of the seat or chair used is important, and consideration should be given to the height of the table or desk on which the drawing board sits. If the board is too low, the calligrapher will inevitably acquire backache through bending over it; if too high, the neck and arms will suffer through constant stretching. The ideal height will differ for each student and adjustments to seating and height of drawing board may be necessary. I even know of one student who uses a foot stool in order to achieve a comfortable working position.

HOLDING THE PEN

It is important to hold the pen correctly between the thumb and first and second fingers, with the third and little fingers bent inwards towards the palm and resting on the writing surface. If this position is totally unnatural or uncomfortable then it may be necessary to resort to the usual method you adopted when writing.

There should be no tenseness and the hold must be relaxed. When writing, minimal pressure is required to form characters and to move the pen. The letterform's thick and thin characteristics are arrived at naturally through both the angle of the nib to the writing line and the direction the pen is moving in. This will be expanded upon with the first alphabet sample.

PEN PRACTICE

It is the angle of the nib in relation to the direction of writing and stroke which gives the letterforms their characteristics. A style that is formed with the nib angle at 30° to the writing line will have a different visual appearance to that lettered at 45°. This is because it is the angle that determines the weight of each stroke and the stress of the round letters. Because the angle is maintained from letter to letter, with the exception of one or two strokes, a certain quality and rhythm is created throughout the letterforms.

Because the pen angle is 30°, a vertical stroke will only be as wide as the image the nib will make at that angle and not equivalent to the full nib width. In a round letterform, there is a point at which the whole of the nib width is used due to the pen travelling in a semicircle.

The maximum width of stroke – 'the stress' – will be exactly 90° to the thinnest stroke, which is fortunate for round letterforms because, if the nature of the tool used did not produce this automatically, round letterforms would appear thinner than vertical ones of the same weight. Indeed, when letterforms are freely constructed with a pencil and filled in with a brush, compensation has to be made to the curved thick strokes,

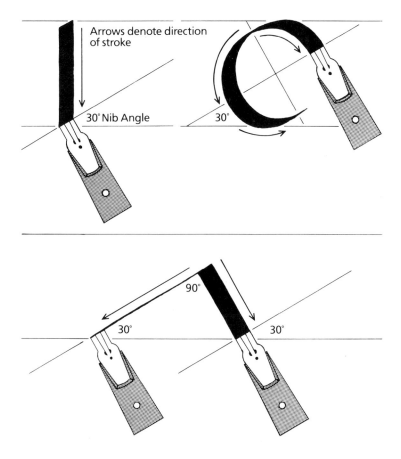

increasing them in weight to give an optical balance with straight strokes.

Weight of stroke is determined by the angle of the pen and the direction of travel. Diagonal strokes will vary in weight depending on the direction of the stroke. Strokes made from top left to bottom right are more consistent than those formed top right to bottom left. Horizontal strokes are of a uniform width. These variations are acceptable in pen lettering and give the forms a natural, unforced appearance. The alphabet is constructed from common vertical, horizontal, diagonal and curved strokes.

Letterforms within the alphabet have common likenesses and, although there are 26 characters, the strokes that are repeated within the capitals and lower case are frequent. This repetition makes the task easier: once the basic strokes used in letter construction are mastered, the forming of individual letters is relatively simple. The ability to produce the strokes with confidence comes from practising them on layout paper.

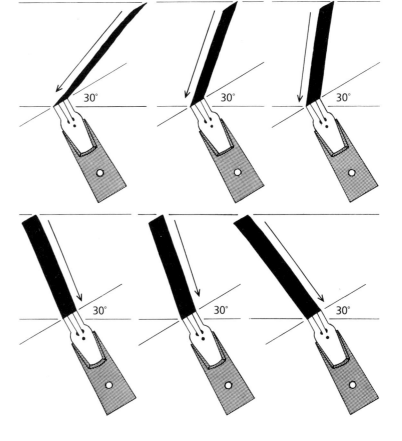

The width of stroke varies according to the direction in which the pen is moved while retaining a fixed nib angle.

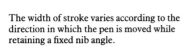

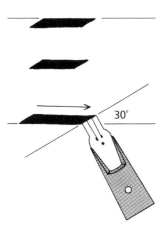

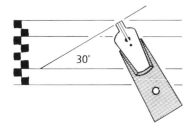

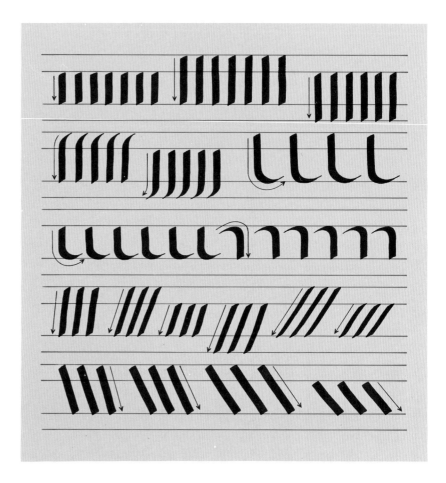

FORMING STROKES

Unlike handwriting, where the pen is lifted from the paper only occasionally between words or necessary breaks in form, calligraphic lettering dictates that the pen is lifted after each stroke. It is the combination of strokes which creates the letterforms.

The pen is nearly always used with a pulling action towards the letterer. Horizontal strokes are made from left to right. The nib should glide across the sheet with just enough pressure to keep it in contact with the writing surface.

It is at this point that problems often face the newcomer to calligraphy. It is essential that the pen angle is maintained while producing the stroke, whatever direction is taken. This usually takes all of the student's concentration and can result in the nib not being in contact with the paper throughout the movement. This skipping will cause an uneven weight in the stroke, and the result will be patchy.

Control over the pen for small letters is with the fingers for the up-and-down movements, with the wrist being employed only slightly for

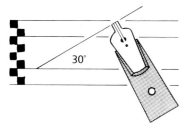

These simple strokes form the basis of letter construction.

rounded letters. When forming larger letters, say over ¾ in (20 mm), the movement is from the shoulder with the whole arm moving down the writing surface. The height of letter at which the transition from finger to arm movement is made is dependent upon the dexterity of the individual.

The exercise requires mainly finger and wrist action with, perhaps, some of the longer, diagonal strokes needing arm movement. The third and little finger rest on the paper and help to support the pen holder.

BASIC LETTER STROKES

Begin by tracing over the forms given in the exercise. To do this, a nib that is of the same size as that used here will be required. Take a nib and compare it with the nib and width of stroke marked at the side of the sample exercise. It will be beneficial if the size can be matched exactly, although a small variation will not matter at this stage. The main aim of the exercise is for the student to become familiar with the action of the pen and to develop a rhythm when forming the images.

25

FROM THUMBNAILS, THROUGH WORKING ROUGH TO FINISHED WORK

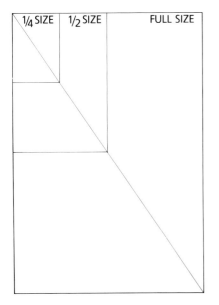

1 Jane Silvester

2 would like you to

2 come to her

birthday party

2 on 24th September

2 at 8pm Flat 3,

2 Long Lane

2 Hampstead,

2 London NW3 (RSVP)
                  3

Deciding on the priorities to be given to lines of text.

If the work is for an invitation card, consider its distribution. If it is to be posted, then there will be a limitation on convenient size. Unless you make the envelope yourself, you will need to know the availability of envelopes and matching paper or card. Check with a stationer which envelopes are available in small quantities to avoid having to use the same envelope and paper again and again. I have chosen a card that measures 4¼ in (105 mm) by 5⅞ in (149 mm) (or A6), which fits into a C6 envelope.

Is the invitation formal or informal? This will determine the type of layout chosen. Centred layouts are generally used for formal occasions but a ranged-left layout can be equally elegant. The use of a ranged-right layout in this instance would be unsuitable, because the work entailed in producing such a layout is too great for lettering a large number of cards. A justified layout can also be disregarded as this is used only for continuous text. An asymmetrical layout could be used for an informal card, if desired. I have decided that the copy can be treated in an informal manner and have chosen to use a ranged-left layout.

Before a rough layout can be made, it must be decided which elements should be prominent. I have underlined the words that I feel should have impact, with remaining copy being coded 1, 2 and 3 in order of importance.

Large-sized lettering, which makes up display headings, attracts the attention of the reader. Secondary information should be smaller than the display but in a size that can be read easily. Subsidiary details can be lettered smaller. The aim of the calligrapher is not only to produce a tasteful letterform but also to lead the reader through the information in a sequence that relates to the order of importance of the text.

In the sample copy, I have underlined the words 'Birthday Party', as I feel these are the key words. The person's name I have given code 1, the invitation text, time and place have code 2 and finally 'RSVP' receives code 3, as it is the least important.

The next step is to rough out some basic ideas in pencil before using pen and ink. This initial work is done on layout paper at a size scaled down from the finished invitation. In this instance half the size is adequate to become familiar with the words and to create an interesting layout by committing any initial thoughts to paper. Rough layouts should be both landscape and portrait formats to discover which shape accepts the text more readily and uses the area to its best advantage.

Begin by drawing some vertical and horizontal boxes in pencil, scaled down to represent the card. To achieve this, draw the card on a piece of layout paper and divide the rectangular box diagonally from the top left-hand corner to the bottom right-hand corner. Then divide the top line of the box into two; on my card this measures 2⅛ in (52.5 mm) to the centre line. Draw a vertical line down from this centre point to where the vertical line meets the diagonal. This is the depth of the card at half-scale. Then draw a horizontal line from the diagonal to the left-hand vertical. The area just defined is a half-size of the original card area. Naturally at a half-size, the measurements could just be divided in half and a rectangle drawn, but on a larger format, where it may be necessary to work on roughs a sixth or an eighth of the original size, this method saves time and calculations. It is also useful when scaling illustrations or drawings up or down. This is

Some initial small roughs to decide on layout.

Jane Silvester
would like you to come to her
Birthday Party
on 24th Sepember at 8pm
at Flat 3, Long Lane,
Hampstead, London NW3

R.S.V.P.

JANE SILVESTER
would like you to come to her
BIRTHDAY PARTY
on 24th September at 8pm
at Flat 3, Long Lane,
Hampstead, London NW3

R.S.V.P.

JANE SILVESTER
would like you to come
to her
Birthday Party
on 24th September at 8pm
at Flat 3, Long Lane,
Hampstead, London NW3   RSVP

Jane Silvester
would like you to come to her
Birthday Party
on 24th September at 8pm
at Flat 3, Long Lane,
Hampstead, London NW3
R.S.V.P.

JANE SILVESTER
would like you
to come to her
BIRTHDAY PARTY
on 24th September
at 8pm
at Flat 3
Long Lane,
Hampstead,
London NW3
R.S.V.P.

Jane Silvester
would like you to
come to her
Birthday Party on 24th
September
at 8pm
at Flat 3, Long Lane,
Hampstead,
London NW3
R.S.V.P.

Birthday Party
Jane Silvester
would like you
to come to her
Birthday Party
on 24 September
at 8pm
at Flat 3
Long Lane,
Hampstead,
London NW3
R.S.V.P.

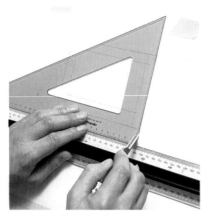
Drawing up the card area.

Lettering 'Birthday Party' using guidelines.

discussed in more detail in the illustrations section.

Begin by using the margins discussed in the previous section, that is, one unit at the head and side margins and 1½ units at the foot. However, it is important to remember that for the roughs these margins must be half-size to keep the same proportion. It may be advisable to reduce the foot margin as the format is quite small and, provided there is more space at the foot than the head, this is quite in order. The text should be placed optically in the depth of the card. Then, using an HB pencil sharpened to a chisel edge, begin to describe the text on the rough layouts (also known as thumbnails owing to their small size).

From the rough layouts I have chosen to use the landscape format that has 'Birthday Party' lettered diagonally across the card. The angle has been fixed at the point at which the italicized letters coincide with the vertical edges of the text area. I feel that this gives stability to the layout and a reference point for the eye.

The rough now requires 'working up'. This is a term which refers to lettering out sample lines which one hopes will fit the working layout. We need to know that the rough will work at actual size before the finished card can be lettered. From the small rough, an intelligent guess can be made as to the nib sizes to use by multiplying the stroke width by two, remembering the roughs were half size. I have decided to try a B4 nib for the display lettering and an Italic Medium for the main text.

The layout is divided into three main parts, commencing with the person's name and the words of the invitation itself, then the event, and finally the venue. The main display line holds the text together and determines how large the main copy can be.

It is first necessary to draw up the card area and borders on a sheet of layout paper, but full-size this time. Start by lettering the display heading in Informal Script with the B4 on a separate piece of layout paper, having first marked out the guidelines by stepping off nib widths, then drawing in the lines with a sharp 2H pencil. Once this has been lettered it should

The words being checked against the text area for line length.

Closing up the letter spacing.

Checking that the reduced letter spaced words fit the text area.

Using a second sheet of tracing paper over the lettered text to mark off line lengths.

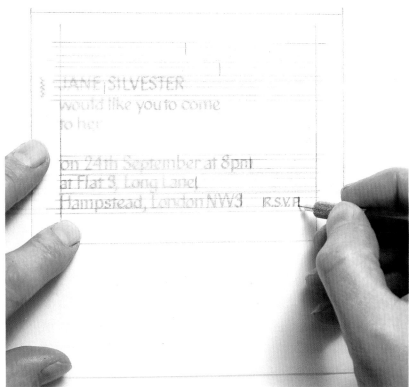

Beginning to letter the text.

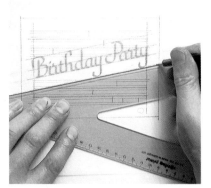

Positioning 'Birthday Party' and marking out guidelines.

be measured against the layout, to check that the line length is correct. If it is overrunning the measure, an adjustment to letter and word spacing may avoid changing to a smaller nib.

Once the heading fits satisfactorily, the main text is then tackled. Step off the nib widths and draw in the guidelines. I have allowed a half-nib-width interlinear space in the event of descenders and ascenders clashing, and also space between the first three lines and the second three lines. After lettering the text, compare it to the layout and mark off the guidelines from the top margin for the first batch of text and from the foot margin for the second. A vertical pencil mark at the end of each line will help to gauge if lines and letters clash when the Italic line is checked against the layout.

Position the heading between the two sections of text. If it is found that there is insufficient room, use some of the extra space from the foot margin by lowering the second batch of copy. Once the position of the Italic line has been established, the guidelines should be transferred to the layout sheet.

A working layout now exists, although admittedly it consists of guidelines only. It is prudent to letter in the text by tracing over the existing lines of copy before turning to the production of the finished card. There may still be some modifications to make; after all the preliminary work it is satisfying to see the completed working layout.

The finished working layout.

Taking measurements from the working layout.

Transferring guidelines to the workpiece using a marker gauge.

On viewing the finished layout, I have decided to range the 'RSVP' to the right so that it aligns with the 'y' in 'party'. I feel this will be visually more pleasing.

The designed layout is then ready to be transferred to the chosen card, which must be slightly larger than the finished size, with a minimum of ½ in (12 mm) selvedge all round, to allow for taping the card to the drawing board. It will be trimmed off when the work is completed. The card size, margin lines and guidelines should be drawn using an HB or H pencil, being careful not to gouge tramlines into the surface – a light line is all that is required. First draw the format area, then, after stepping off the margins and guidelines on a strip of cartridge paper, transfer them to the card. The diagonal lines will have to be marked from both left- and right-hand margins.

Before beginning to letter, it is necessary to consider the colour in which the text will be written – black is hardly party-like. I have chosen peach-coloured card, with red ink for the words 'Birthday Party' and blue ink for the remaining text. A small piece of card was put to one side for trial lettering and colour checking. It is always useful to have an extra piece of the chosen material, because the action of the pen and ink may differ from surface to surface.

Position the card on the writing line, that is, the lettering position at which the student feels comfortable on the board. Tape it into position and cover with a guard sheet, leaving only the first line visible. Taking the working layout, make a fold just above the x line and position it so that the first line is just below the descender line of the first guidelines on the card. Letter the line and repeat the procedure until all the lines have been worked.

It may help to reposition the piece of work after lettering the first three lines. I personally find that it is easier to move the guard downwards for a small piece of work, where only a small deviation from the writing line is required. However, when lettering a deep column of text it is better to

Drawing guidelines on to the workpiece.

Testing various inks for colour compatibility.

Lettering out the text using a guard sheet to keep the work surface clean.

JANE SILVESTER
would like you to come
to her

on 24th September at 8pm
at Flat 3, Long Lane,
Hampstead, London NW3   R.S.V.P.

The main text completed.

Lettering in 'Birthday Party'.

leave the guard in the writing position and move the workpiece, which need not be taped to the drawing-board surface.

To letter the Italic line, the card should be turned until the text is horizontal to the writing line. The finished card should be put to one side to give the ink time to dry before removing the guidelines. This is done with a plastic eraser rather than a normal rubber eraser because it is kinder to both ink and lettering surface.

Erasing the guidelines once the ink has thoroughly dried.

Trimming the card to size, with a blade, on the waste side of the ruler.

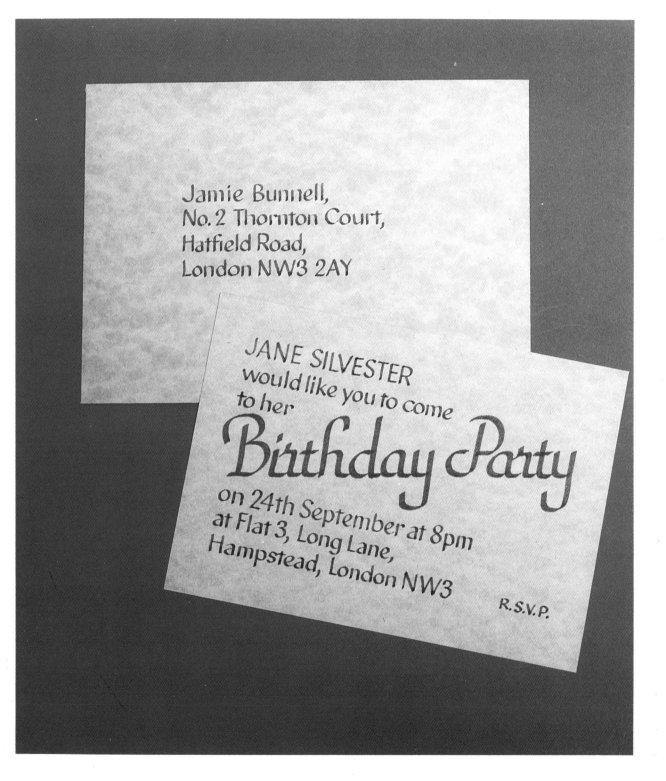

CALLIGRAPHY AND ILLUSTRATIONS

When combining illustration with calligraphy, it is important to create harmony between both elements. The illustration should reflect the square-edged pen, as do many early manuscripts, with line drawings making full use of the implement and the varied stroke widths it will produce. Textures can be built up by cross hatching (strokes in opposing directions) or by moving the pen angle from a thin stroke gradually through to a thick stroke position and vice-versa, giving a vignetted (gentle graduation of) line weight.

There is no easy way to learn how to draw with a square nib, and if, like myself, the student does not regard himself as an illustrator the only way to succeed is by involvement and practice. I have spent many years analyzing woodcuts, and they have given me inspiration for various projects as they adapt well to the pen. Thomas Bewick produced some of the finest woodcuts known and turned wood-engraving into an art form.

I would suggest, when considering illustrative work, that the student obtain photographic or printed references before commencing. Once he has an idea of the image he wishes to accompany a piece of calligraphy, he should search his own or a local library for suitable images or photographs, books and pamphlets. Searching for material will heighten the student's awareness of the images he sees every day. I store away illustrative references like gold dust, with any image I feel that may be remotely useful tagged in books or magazines for future use. A scrapbook of likely subject matter is a wonderful idea and takes very little time to add to each week. References should be as detailed as possible so that new images can readily and accurately be created from them.

I learnt my lesson some years ago when employed by a leading auction house. I was asked to produce a poster for a sale which included prints of bicycles. The print chosen for the image of the poster was slightly soiled and faded and depicted a man riding a penny farthing. I duly produced a drawing for the printers, but when the posters arrived I realized, to my horror, that the front wheel of my penny farthing would never have

Tracing the image to be used from illustrative reference.

Shading over the underside of the tracing.

Tracing the image on to the finished surface.

Inking in the initial outline.

The finished illustration.

turned because of my positioning of the front pedal. Very early days in my career, and a mistake which fortunately only I had noticed. With more adequate reference it could have been avoided, but it taught me to check carefully the images I create.

Once the necessary references have been found, the student will need to transfer them to tracing paper. If the size of the illustration required is the same as that of the reference material, it can be traced directly on to the

Confining the illustration to a gridded square on tracing paper.

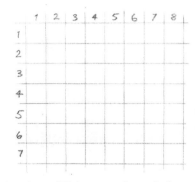

Drawing a gridded square to the required enlargement.

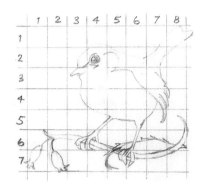

Plotting the image on the grid.

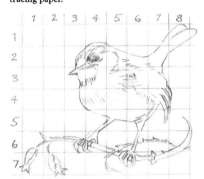

Building up the illustration.

Shading over the underside of the tracing.

Tracing the image on to the finished surface.

Traced image on finished surface.

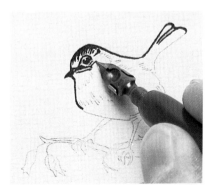

Inking in the initial outline.

The finished illustration.

tracing paper, using a 2H or H pencil (or lead in a technical pencil). Take care to interpret the image exactly, because what is produced on the tracing sheet will be the image traced down on to the finished piece of work. Once the tracing is completed, the sheet must be turned over and the underside of the drawing area shaded over with an HB pencil. Turn the tracing paper over again so that the image side faces upwards and position it on the finished surface of the work using masking tape at the

Some designs which I have used for bookmarks and Christmas cards.

head (top) to hold it gently in place. Then trace the drawing down by going over the lines of the image using a hard, sharp pencil, 2H or 4H. When completed, lift the tracing sheet, without unfastening, to make sure that the drawing has been successfully transferred to the finished surface. The faint image must now be inked in with a fine, square-ended nib. Build up the image slowly, referring to the original reference for the finer points.

Should the reference material found not be the correct size for the design, then it will be necessary either to enlarge or reduce the image. First contain the illustration within a square or rectangle on a sheet of tracing paper, subdividing this by small grid squares. The size required should then be drawn as a square or rectangle on another sheet and subdivided as before. Number the squares horizontally and vertically on both sheets of paper and plot your image from the reference material to the correctly-sized grid.

Signs of the zodiac. Some have been taken from English and German woodcuts and adapted for the pen. The Crab, Scorpion and Scales are my additions, as the originals were not suitable to be contained within a circle. The shading in the lower portion was necessary to give a uniformity to the twelve symbols.

RULES AND BORDERS

Decorative elements have been used to complement letterforms for almost as long as the written word has existed. Early manuscripts display decorative initials so elaborate in form as to lose the legibility of the character being embellished. Common sense and restraint must prevail and decorative enhancement play only a secondary role to that of communication. All a student's efforts therefore should be directed towards maintaining legibility while retaining harmony between text and illustrative work. I feel this is of paramount importance if the work is to be functional as opposed to just clever or fashionable.

Before applying decoration to a piece of calligraphy, question its relevance. Does the text require embellishing? There may be good reasons for adding a border, tailpiece, swelled rule, box rule, cartouche or similar device. Short rules are often introduced as divisions between sections of text, on menus for instance. Tailpieces are regularly seen as ornamentation at the beginning or ending of chapters; and box rules or borders assist in emphasising sections of text. They all have their applications, but over-indulgence can result in the original message being overpowered by fanciful imagery.

When combining calligraphy with rules and borders, spare a thought for the compatibility between the letterform and the ornamentation. As letter styles have their place in periods of history, so too does decoration. Black Letter text with a 1920s or 1930s border would not be appropriate.

If asked to produce work that requires the use of borders, search a central library under the printing section. Sufficient reference will be found there not only for samples of 'flowers', 'arabesques', 'rules' and 'borders' (these are primarily printing terms), but also for the appropriate period to which they belong.

Alternatively the student can design his own borders. Do not be put off by thinking they are too complicated, as most borders, once analyzed, can be easily reproduced, since they are based on the repetition of basic designs. For example, a simple border can be designed around a 'flower' (the decorative unit) and be contained within a square measuring seven nib widths by seven nib widths. This could be subdivided to give reference points for the beginning and ending of the various elements within the flower. This border may also require a 45° corner device, as it is

Deciding on the proportions of the flower.

Designing the corner device.

Transferring the unit values to a strip of card.

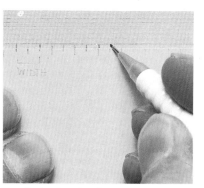

Transferring the values from the card to the finished surface.

The finished border used as an 'Ex Libris' for a friend's library.

38

Useful decorative items for the calligrapher: some borders, a cartouche, swelled rules and a tailpiece.

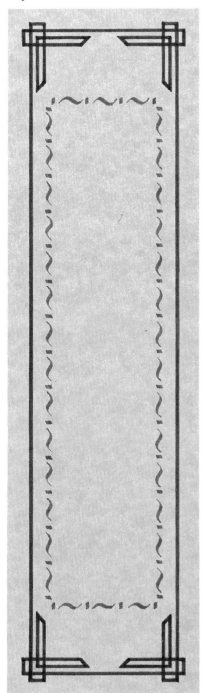

not symmetrical, and possibly the foot of the flower might face inwards on each side of the border. The size of the border is established by multiplying the width and depth of the decorative unit respectively.

For the cartouche and the tailpiece in a large border, preliminary work is carried out on tracing paper. Only a half or quarter of the image requires developing as the repetition is achieved by inverting or mirror-imaging the original drawing when tracing down on the finished surface.

INDEX